Anderson Public Library
Lawrenceburg, KY 40342

WITHDRAWN

JUV 031 Ripl

Beyond understanding.

DEC 2 3 2009

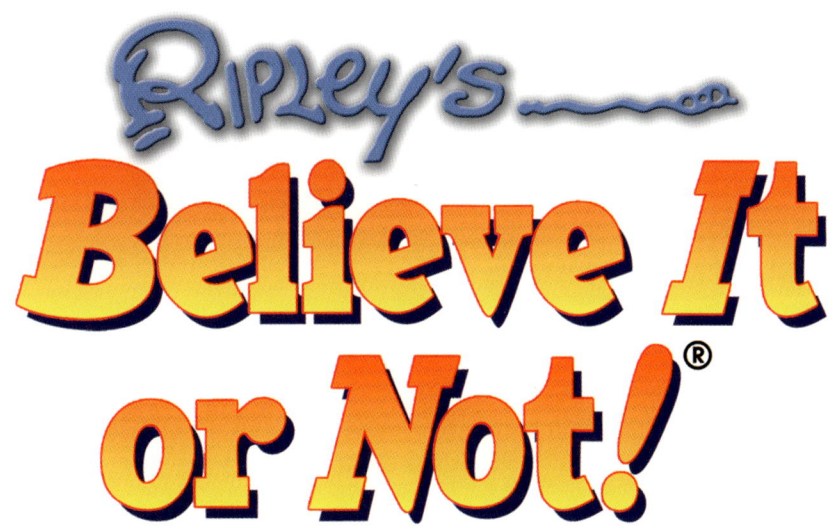

Developed and produced by Ripley Publishing Ltd

This edition published and distributed by:
Mason Crest Publishers Inc.
370 Reed Road, Broomall, Pennsylvania 19008
(866) MCP-BOOK (toll free)
www.masoncrest.com

Copyright © 2004 by Ripley Entertainment Inc. This edition printed in 2009.
All rights reserved. Ripley's, Believe It or Not!, and Ripley's Believe It or Not!
are registered trademarks of Ripley Entertainment Inc.

Ripley's Believe It or Not!
Beyond Understanding
ISBN 978-1-4222-1531-9
Library of Congress Cataloging-in-Publication data is available

Ripley's Believe It or Not!—Complete 16 Title Series
ISBN 978-1-4222-1529-6

No part of this publication may be reproduced in whole or in part, or stored in a retrieval
system, or transmitted in any form or by any means, electronic, mechanical,
photocopying, recording, or otherwise, without written permission from the publishers.
For information regarding permission, write to VP Intellectual Property, Ripley
Entertainment Inc., Suite 188, 7576 Kingspointe Parkway, Orlando, Florida, 32819
email: publishing@ripleys.com

PUBLISHER'S NOTE
While every effort has been made to verify the accuracy of the entries in this book,
the Publishers cannot be held responsible for any errors contained in the work.
They would be glad to receive any information from readers.

WARNING
Some of the stunts and activities in this book are undertaken by experts and should not
be attempted by anyone without adequate training and supervision.

Printed in the United States of America

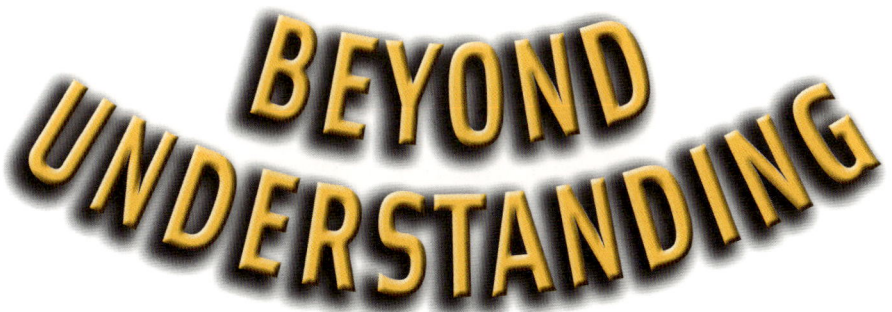

a Jim Pattison Company

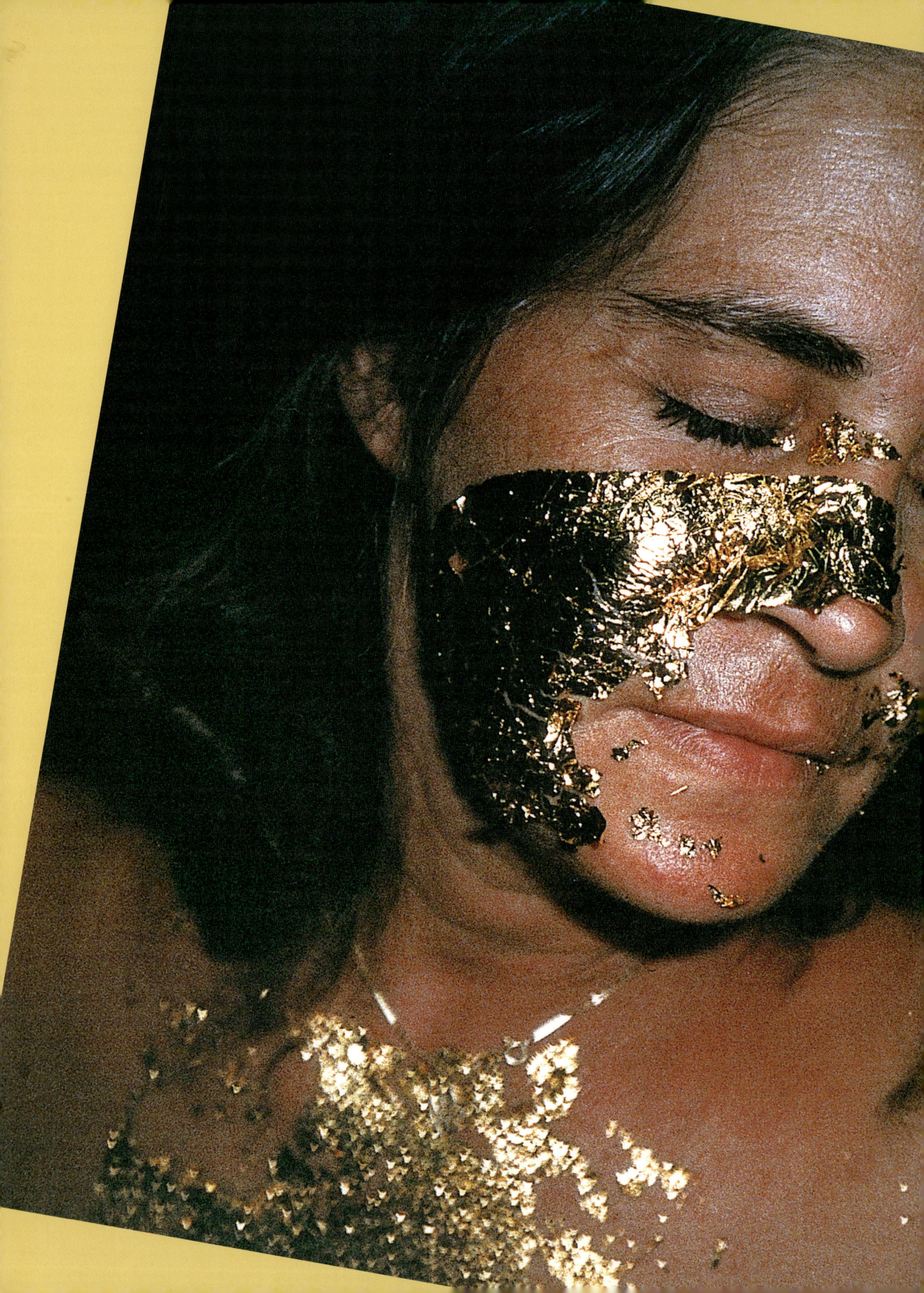

Beyond Understanding

is a collection of astonishing facts, legends, and stories about a range of inexplicable phenomena. Read about the Chinese moon landing 4,000 years ago, the ghost gardeners of the Palace of Versailles, and a winged cat—all in this remarkable book.

A psychic, named Katie, displayed the ability to grow copper on her skin...

Earth's Nightlight

If humans had been around in the very earliest years of the Earth's life, nights would have been very dark for them indeed—because there was no moonlight at all.

In fact, there was no Moon. Amazingly, the Moon did not form at the same time as the Earth, but some time after. Scientists think the Moon formed when another small planet cannoned into the newborn Earth—with an impact so tremendous it melted almost instantly. Just like a stone hurled into a pond, the impact flung splashes of melted planet back out into space. As the splashes cooled down, they clumped together to form the Moon.

If you wanted to see all of Australia, Europe, and America in less than a half day, you could try sitting on the Moon. The Moon barely moves, but the Earth spins round beneath it at over 24,860 mph (40,000 km/h)!

MOON MATTERS

- With gravity just a sixth of the Earth's, the average person on the Moon could jump 13 ft (4 m) straight up—like jumping on top of a double-decker bus!

- The Sun shines for up to 360 hours on the Moon's sunny side and temperatures can reach up to 260°F (127°C)

- The Moon looks the same size as the Sun but at a staggering 870,000 mi (1.4 million km) across, the Sun is 400 times bigger than the Moon, which is just 2,175 mi (3,500 km) across. Yet at a distance of 93 million mi (150 million km) from us, the Sun is 400 times farther away than the Moon, which is just 240,000 mi (384,000 km) away

Beyond Understanding

The footprints left behind on the Moon by Apollo astronauts, Neil Armstrong and Edwin "Buzz" Aldrin, more than 30 years ago are still there—just as perfect as if they were made yesterday, because there is no wind or rain to ever wipe them away. In fact, they will probably last forever.

High and Dry
The Moon is covered in scores of seas, known as maria (the Latin for sea)—yet there is not a drop of water in any of them, nor has there ever been. They just looked like seas to early astronomers on Earth. The first manned mission to the Moon landed in the bone-dry Sea of Tranquillity.

Hollow Claim In 1976, two Russian scientists claimed that the Moon is not a natural satellite of Earth but a "hollowed-out planetoid fashioned by a highly advanced, technologically sophisticated civilization into an artificial 'inside out' world which was steered into orbit around the Earth eons ago."

First Moon Landing? According to Chinese historical tradition, a man and a woman landed on the Moon over 4,000 years ago. The engineer Hou-Yih and his wife, Chang Ngo, flew to the Moon on a celestial bird. Their descriptions of the conditions on the Moon were incredibly accurate. Was their journey the result of an over-active imagination or did they really go there using technology that was later lost to mankind?

Long Shot When man landed on the Moon, David Trelfall won US$18,000. In 1964, he placed a bet, on odds of 1,000 to 1, that a man would set foot on the Moon before January 1, 1971.

Far Sighted View A voyage to the moon by ship was described in a work of fiction by Lucian of Samasota, Syria, in the 2nd century CE.

Moon in the Window A piece of Moon rock is enshrined in the stained glass window of Washington Cathedral.

Aztec Astronomy A calendar wheel used by the ancient Aztecs of Mexico traced the intricate orbits of the Earth and Moon and accurately forecasted eclipses.

Good Vibes After the crew of *Apollo 12* landed on the Moon, in 1969, the lunar surface continued to vibrate for almost an hour.

> "More than 450 astronauts have traveled into space"

Since the world's first artificial satellite, the Russian Sputnik 1, *was launched into space in 1957, there have been over 4,000 successful launches of spacecraft—manned missions of exploration, robot probes to distant planets, orbiting space laboratories, and satellites.*

Firepower

Every second, the Sun gives out enough energy to supply all the United States' energy needs for 50 million years! To produce this, it burns up an incredible 4 million tons of its mass. However, it will take about 5 billion years to burn it all up, so we needn't worry about it running out. The weight of the Sun is 332,946 times that of the Earth and it burns up some 33 billion million tons of hydrogen in a year.

The Sun burns so brilliantly that it lights the Earth with daylight, even though it is over 93 million mi (150 million km) away. In fact, every square inch of the Sun's surface—no bigger than a postage stamp—burns with the brightness of over 1.5 million candles!

Hard Nosed The Danish astronomer Tycho Brahe had an artificial nose of solid metal. His real nose was cut off in a duel in 1566, when he was 20.

Rounded View The first person to suggest that the Earth was not flat, but actually spherical, was the Greek philosopher Philolaus of Tarentum in 450 BC.

Near Miss Our world was almost destroyed by an asteroid in 1976. The asteroid in orbit around the Sun was only 750,000 mi (1.2 million km) away, which, in space terms, is too close for comfort!

BLIND SPOTS
The first observation of sunspots had to be kept secret! They were observed by a Jesuit, Father Scheiner, in 1650 but it would have been blasphemous to acknowledge the fact because the Sun was regarded as the purest symbol of celestial incorruptibility.

Great Balls of Fire Balls of fire have been witnessed through the ages. Scientists call them "ball lightning" but no one knows what they are or how they are produced. Some cause damage but most do not and they appear to be able to pass through solid objects without harming them.

Implosion When the gravity of a star becomes too great, it collapses in upon itself. Sometimes this imploding increases until absolutely nothing can escape its force. When it reaches this stage it is known as a "black hole."

Starlets Not all stars shine. Nor are they all gigantic. In fact, there are stars out in space that are completely dark and smaller than the Moon. They can be just 17–23 mi (27–37 km) across, no bigger than a large city, and are called neutron stars because they are made almost entirely from subatomic particles called neutrons.

Light Speed It takes 8 minutes for the light of the Sun to reach Earth.

Serious Size The star Sirius is about 25 times brighter than our Sun.

Universal Age The Universe is between 12 and 15 billion years old.

Massive Crater The largest known meteorite crater, the Chixulub crater in Mexico, is 112 mi (180 km) across!

The Barringer crater in Arizona was caused by a meteorite that hit Earth 25,000 to 40,000 years ago! It is 2,625 ft (800 m) across and 656 ft (200 m) deep.

Beyond Understanding

Comets streaking across the heavens were once thought to be warnings from the gods of war, plague, famine, or death—and when any occurred in a comet year (the year a comet appears), it was thought to be proof positive—even though worse things often happened in non-comet years!

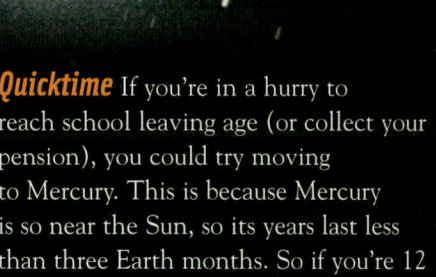

Long Wait The Delavan comet returns to our Solar System every 24 million years!

Space Diet If you really want to lose weight, you could move to Pluto. This is because Pluto is small and its gravity weak, so you would weigh just two-thirds of what you do on Earth. However, if you went to Jupiter, you would weigh 23 times as much!

Pocket Stars At just 10 mi (16 km) across—no bigger than a small town—the smallest stars of all are strange or quark stars, discovered in 2002, and made entirely from quarks, the tiniest subatomic particles of all.

Pioneer Guppies South American guppies were the first fish in space.

Quicktime If you're in a hurry to reach school leaving age (or collect your pension), you could try moving to Mercury. This is because Mercury is so near the Sun, so its years last less than three Earth months. So if you're 12 on Earth now, you'd be nearly 50 years old on Mercury!

Earliest Atoms Atoms were first described by the Greek intellectual, Democritus of Addesa, over 2,000 years ago.

Closing the Circle

Around 250 BCE the Greek philosopher Eratosthenes of Cyrene worked out the circumference of the Earth from shadows! He observed that shadows cast by the Sun at two places 500 mi (800 km) apart differed by seven degrees. From this he calculated that if Earth were a sphere and the seven degree difference equalled 500 mi (800 km) then its circumference was about 25,000 mi (40,230 km) and its diameter about 8,000 mi (12,875 km). He was incredibly close, for we now know that the circumference is 24,902.4 mi (40,075 km) and the average diameter (because the Earth is not an exact sphere) is 7,917.78 mi (12,740 km).

Super Dense Neutron stars are so compressed that they squeeze a tenth of the matter that made up the original giant star (before it imploded) into a ball 1.5 billion times smaller.

Cubic Weight Neutron stars are so dense that a fragment the size of a sugar cube would weigh as much as all the people on Earth put together.

Tight Ball At just 20 mi (32 km) across, the average neutron star packs one tenth of the amount of matter as the Sun into only a billionth of the space.

Whirling Stars Spinning at more than 1,000 times a second, some neutron stars rotate ten times faster than a compact disc.

Sunny Days Our Solar System is about 4.6 billion years old.

Two amazed, and rather scared Russian farm workers, Anna Takhtarova and her granddaughter Rita, were the first people to meet Yuri Gagarin when he landed on Earth in his landing apparatus (shown here) after the world's first ever manned space flight in April 1961.

Moonlight Magic By Columbus

The discovery of America might not have been announced had it not been for an eclipse of the Moon. Knowing that an eclipse was due, Columbus announced to hostile natives in Jamaica that he would make the Moon "lose her light." When it happened as predicted, the natives caused no more trouble and Columbus eventually sailed back to Europe to announce his discoveries.

Pulling Power Neutron stars called magnetars may be a million times smaller than the Earth, but they have a thousand trillion times the magnetic power!

Heavenly Beat Like the flashing lights on police cars, pulsars are neutron stars that send out signals in regular pulses because they rotate at high speed.

Spaceman's Breakfast Before he entered the *Vostok 1* spacecraft on April 12, 1961, Yuri Gagarin had chopped meat, blackberry jam, and coffee for breakfast.

Happy Birthday Apollo 9 astronauts sang "Happy Birthday to You," in space for the first on March 8, 1969.

Space Hop America's first manned space venture lasted only 15 minutes, 22 seconds. The 302-mi (483-km) sub-orbital flight was made in the Mercury spacecraft, *Freedom 7*, by astronaut Alan B. Shepherd on May 5, 1961.

Weightless Tummy The medical kits that were issued to America's *Skylab* crew included pills intended to control travel sickness.

Greetings on High "Capriadno was vidit" were the first words spoken by an American to a Russian the first time they met in space in 1975. They mean "How nice to see you again" and were spoken by the American General Tom Stafford to Russian Colonel Alexei Leonov when an *Apollo* spaceship docked with a *Soyuz* spaceship.

A former tire factory worker was the first woman in space—Valentina Tereshkova. In the late 1950s Tereshkova took up parachuting and in 1960 was selected for space training, becoming the first woman in space just two years later.

Flashy Rings

Made entirely of light gases such as hydrogen and helium, the planet Saturn is so light it would actually float—if you could find a swimming pool big enough! Saturn is 1,000 times as big as the Earth but less than 100 times as heavy. Saturn is the farthest planet from the Earth that we can sometimes see with the naked eye. Although the other planets can be seen from Earth they do not emit any light. The light that enables us to see them is reflected sunlight. The amount of sunlight decreases as it travels through the Solar System so the planets beyond Saturn are so faint they are not visible to the naked eye.

It has been suggested that the pygmies of the Ituri Forest in Central Africa called Saturn "the star of the nine moons"—before scientists even knew about Saturn's moons!

Encounters of the Alien Kind!

Alien Panic
An invasion of Earth by aliens on October 30, 1936, caused a panic in America. Telephone systems were jammed with people phoning the police, hospitals, newspapers, relatives, and friends for advice or to pass on the news they were hearing from their radio. The broadcast, presented in the form of a live story, was actually a play adapted by the actor Orson Welles, from H.G. Wells' novel *The War of the Worlds*.

A short drive in New Hampshire in 1961 took seven hours out of two people's lives!

Betty and Barney Hill were confused about why it had taken them so long to reach their destination. However, it wasn't until two years later when they sought the advice of psychiatrist Dr. Benjamin Simon to deal with their reccuring and strangely similar nightmares, that they were hypnotized to get to the root of their night-time stirrings. While hypnotized, they both told how they had been pulled from their car by strange beings and subjected to intense medical examination. Betty, in her hypnotic state, also told how the origin of the aliens was the Zeta Reticuli, which is a star system in space. It was not actually officially discovered until 1969!

Betty and Barney Hill were the first people to speak out in public about their apparent alien encounter, and since then, many other "abductees" have stepped forward to speak of their similar experiences.

Flying Pancakes Joe Simonton said he met aliens in 1961 and they gave him several salt-free pancakes. Joe was thereafter nicknamed "Pancake Joe."

Fellow Traveler George Adamski, a hotdog seller at the Mount Palomar Observatory near San Diego, California, claimed that he made many contacts with beings from other worlds and even flew with them throughout the Solar System. His first contact was apparently near Desert Center, Arizona, on November 20, 1952.

Dead Language The Martian written language was first copied down by Catherine Muller of Geneva, Switzerland, who insisted she learned it from a departed associate during a seance.

Ripley's Believe It or Not!

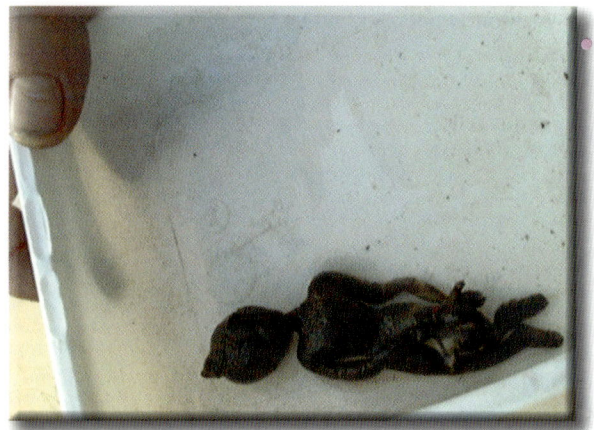

This strange creature was discovered in northern Israel in 1998. At 4–5 in (10–12 cm), it has what appear to be arms, legs, fingers, and a head. Many believe that this strange creature was an alien.

Real Saucers Just Won't Fly
Just before 1960, the Canadian government financed a program to build an advanced flying saucer. This jet-power disc would fly incredibly fast—1,500 mph (2,414 km/h)—and take off and land vertically. However, the project became so expensive that it was sold to the U.S.A. for further development. Unfortunately, the craft proved unstable at speeds above 30 mph (48 km/h), and could not rise higher than 4 ft (1 m) without tipping dangerously.

Group Sighting More than 50 people confirmed the sighting of an object that flew around Trindade Island in the South Atlantic on January 16, 1958. The crew of the Brazilian Hydrographic and Navigation Service vessel, the *Alminante Saldanha*, and a team of divers on board claimed to have seen the object.

True Believers A poll revealed that 92 percent of Americans believe that aliens are living among us.

Official Stamp Equatorial Guinea was the first country to depict flying saucers on its stamps.

Hot Craft Carl Farlow was driving a truck between Avon and Sopley, in Britain, on November 6, 1967 when the vehicle's lights went out. An oval object floated across the road then flew away and disappeared. Police later discovered that it had burned the ground, melting the pavement.

Letter from Mars The letter B on the side of a Martian rock was clearly seen when a Viking space probe transmitted pictures of the surface of Mars to Earth in 1976. The Pasadena Space Center was inundated with telephone calls about this apparent evidence of life on the red planet.

UFO Triggered Crash American pilot Captain Thomas Mantell chased an unidentified flying object at Godman Air Force Base, Kentucky, on January 7, 1948. During the chase Mantell's plane exploded and the wreckage was found 90 mi (145 km) away. The official explanation was that the pilot had been chasing the planet Venus, but it was later shown that Venus was not visible at that time.

The Mystery of Roswell?
In July 1947, a mysterious object crashed in a remote part of New Mexico. A local rancher from the town of Roswell reported to the sheriff that he might have recovered the remains of a flying saucer. The sheriff promptly reported this to the nearby military airbase, which sent out a team to examine the wreckage. The world was soon astonished by an official report telling of the recovery of the remains of a "flying disc." By the next day, the military were officially denying everything and claimed that it was just the remains of a weather balloon. The actual remains were of shiny metallic plastic material, but they seem to have disappeared since. From then on, argument has raged about the significance of the incident.

This is alledgedly the remains of the "flying disc" that landed in Roswell in July 1947. However, many believe it to be material from a weather balloon.

Beyond Understanding

Nazi Secret Weapon In 1959, reports leaked out that the Nazi regime had created several mysterious flying discs, which were said to have phenomenal performance, though no evidence of their existence was ever found. They were said to have been designed by several scientists: Schreiver, Miethe, Bellonzo, and Habermohl, although none of these individuals was ever traced after the war. One such flying disc certainly existed. It was designed by German farmer, Arthur Sack, and tested by Luftwaffe pilots in 1944. Unfortunately, it was very reluctant to leave the ground and the project was abandoned!

Saucer Eyes While flying over the Cascade Mountains in Washington state on June 24, 1947, pilot Kenneth Arnold saw several shining lights that looked like bat-winged craft. He described them as moving "like a saucer would if you skipped it across the water." That observation coined the term "flying saucer."

Wheel of Light Men on a British steamer sailing through the Persian Gulf in 1906 witnessed an enormous wheel of light revolving under the water. Beams from the wheel, which was bigger than the steamer, passed through the vessel but did not harm it or the crew in any way!

New World? Explorer Christopher Columbus saw a UFO the night before his discovery of the New World.

Paul Villa is a true believer in the existence of alien life. He has spent years photographing what he claims to be UFOs. He sends his photographs to important heads of state, as well as distributing copies to the public. He is determined to one day capture an image of a UFO that he believes will prove, beyond doubt, that UFOs and, consequently, aliens, exist! Meanwhile, people inevitably believe that his photographs are fakes, including this one taken in Albuquerque, New Mexico.

"UFO left grid pattern of dots on chest of American man"

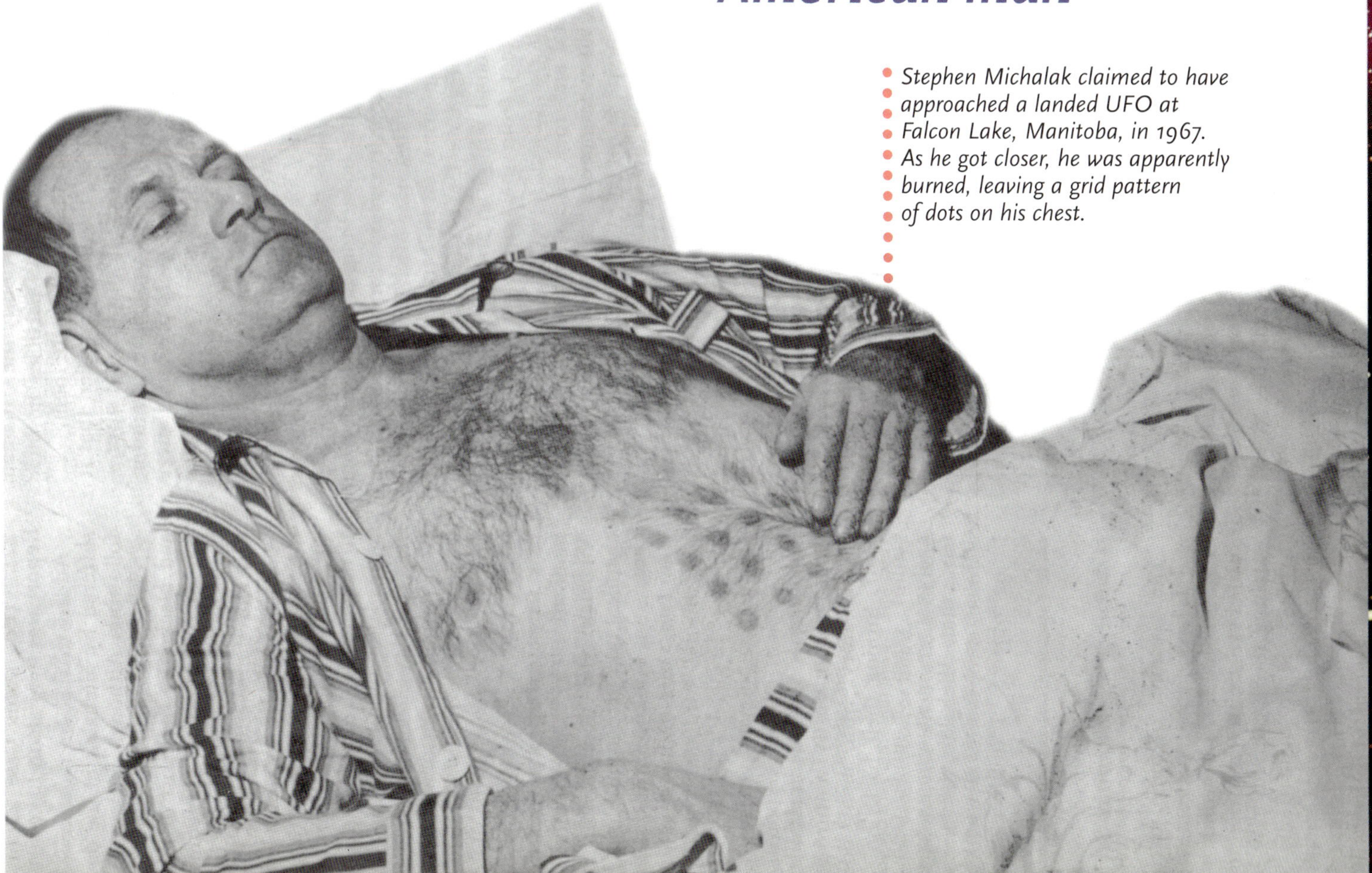

Stephen Michalak claimed to have approached a landed UFO at Falcon Lake, Manitoba, in 1967. As he got closer, he was apparently burned, leaving a grid pattern of dots on his chest.

Ripley's Believe It or Not!

What's Going on in Area 51?
Each working day, at least 500 people are flown in to work at a mysterious base in Nevada, which officially does not exist. This place, called Area 51, is part of the Groom Lake airbase, where the U2 spy plane was first tested in conditions of great secrecy, and where new stealth aircraft are rumored to be tested. Very heavy security keeps curious people away but there are rumors that several alien spacecraft are kept at Area 51 for test purposes, so their workings can be understood and applied to new projects. There have even been reports that a dead alien has been dissected, studied, and contained at this secret base.

Lights Out A red flying object disabled the lights, radio, and engine of a car driven by a schoolteacher in Cochcrane, Wisconsin, on April 3, 1968.

This photograph purports to show an alien that was recovered from a UFO that crashed in 1950 near New Mexico. The "alien" was apparently sent to Germany for examination, but it is believed to be a hoax.

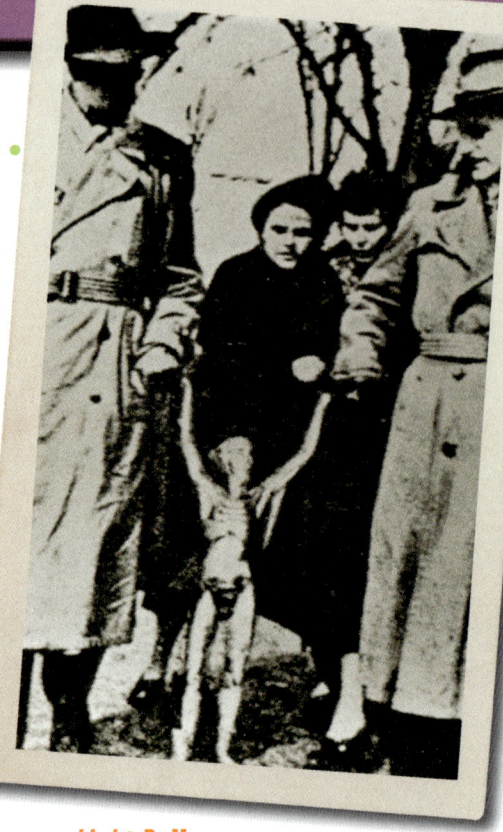

Waving Aliens There were numerous witnesses to the appearance of a strange flying vessel over an Anglican mission in Papua New Guinea in June 1959. Father Gill, the mission staff, and all the congregation saw a circular vessel with rails, "like the bridge of a boat." The crew of four were leaning over the rails and when the people on the ground waved to them, they waved back!

Vanishing Author After a meeting with an alien in February 1954, Cedric Allingham disappeared! The meeting took place near Lossiemouth, Scotland, and Allingham then wrote a book about the event but was then never heard of again!

Light Bells Canadian Second World War soldier Lance Corporal Carson Yorke saw a ball of light floating in the air near Antwerp, Belgium. It was joined by four other glowing balls, but to this day no one knows what they were.

UFOs were apparently sighted in 1989, flying above Russia.

Beyond Understanding   15

Playful Ghosts Go Bump in the Night

There have been many reports of poltergeist activity in countries around the world, terrifying families with their antics.

In 1973, in an ordinary suburban house in Enfield, North London, England, psychic investigators looked into a case of poltergeists (a German word meaning "noisy ghost") who were harassing Peggy Harper, a divorced woman living with her four children. Her children's beds jumped up and down and objects flew about mysteriously. The police were called in, and one police officer reported seeing a chair float into the air. Next, the children floated into the air, too. The poltergeist activity ended suddenly in 1979, at about the same time that one of the girls entered puberty.

This upended furniture in the Webster's living room was apparently the work of a poltergeist. The haunting of this cottage in Chester, England, began in late 1984 and continued for a couple of years. The residents of the cottage tracked the "poltergeist" back to a man named Tomas Harden, who lived in a cottage that was on the same plot of land in the 16th century. The couple had been renovating their property and believe that this disturbed the poltergeist.

In 1985, Ken Webster had a computer in his home, rare for the time, and would often find messages written on the screen from Tomas Harden. The messages were always in an old style of English and would have to be translated to make sense. Not content with writing messages on the computer screen, Harden would often write them on the floor of the cottage as well. Between 1984 and 1987, the Websters received around 300 messages from their poltergeist!

Ripley's Believe It or Not!

The Magic Word The word "abracadabra" was once believed to cure fevers.

Floating Feat Victorian spiritualist Daniel Douglas Home could levitate! Many observers asserted that it was a trick although no one could explain how he did it.

Early Rapper The Fox family of Hydesville, near Rochester, New York, in December 1847 heard knocking coming from the walls of their cottage. They found out that the raps could answer questions, and Kate and Margaretta Fox started giving public demonstrations that led to the Spiritualist movement in America.

Dead Hands Patience Worth wrote novels 150 years after her death! In July 1913, Mrs. Curran received messages through a ouija board, and over the next 15 years the dead Patience Worth wrote four full-length novels and numerous poems through Mrs. Curan.

This headless ghost of a dog was photographed in Buckinghamshire, England, in 1916. The detective inspector who took the photo did not recall seeing the apparition at the time!

At two years old, Greg Sheldon Maxwell often would say "Old Nanna's here" and seemingly point at nothing in particular. When this photograph was developed, it was suggested that the haze in front of him was actually the ghost of his great-grandmother!

Termites Tell The Azande people of Africa use termites to answer questions about future events.

Blast from the Past Ghost gardeners, a man who disappeared, a lady sketching, and an 18th-century wedding were witnessed by two ladies, Charlotte Anne Moberley and Eleanor Jourdain, in the grounds of the Palace of Versailles, France, on August 10, 1901. Five months later they revisited the grounds but the places they had walked through did not exist. They had apparently somehow walked back in time and seen ghosts of the past.

The Spirits of Bull Henry Bull and his family regularly heard ghostly footsteps, a ringing bell, mysterious tapping, and strange voices when they lived at Borley Rectory in Essex, England. In 1892, when Henry Bull's son took over the house, an ethereal coach was seen in the drive and a headless man walked the garden. Later occupants saw scribbled messages appear on the walls.

Ghost Writer In 1998, three workers at a museum in Havana, Cuba, resigned after seeing the ghost of writer Ernest Hemingway.

Blot on the Family
£50,000 ($27,000) was paid by the Muret family of Thionville, France, to a magician to ensure their son's success on his exams. The family were instructed to take part in obscure activities, including drinking ink and balancing eggs on their heads—but the spell failed and the boy came last in the exam results!

Return Flight from Beyond Captain Bob Loft and Second Officer Don Repo were both seen by other pilots in other airplanes after their deaths on December 29, 1972, when they crashed in the Florida Everglades.

Killer Lemons Lemons were used by witches to kill people. The name of your enemy was written on a piece of paper pinned to a lemon. This resulted in him or her becoming ill, going mad, or even dying.

Rough Justice Women in the 17th century were often drowned to prove they were not witches. A suspected witch was bound and thrown into water. If she floated she was deemed to be a witch but if she sank she was innocent —many drowned in the process.

Beyond Understanding

FORTUNE TELLING
- Moleosophy—discovering a person's destiny by "reading" the moles on their body
- Geomancy—using a handful of earth or random dots to tell someone's fate
- Axinomancy—fortune-telling with an ax
- Pessomancy—reading signs created out of patterns of pebbles
- Scapulomancy—using bones to determine someone's destiny

Screaming Skull Ghostly groans and other terrifying noises were heard in Burton Agnes Hall, Bridlington, England, following the death of its 17th-century owner, Anne Griffith. She had asked for her head to be kept in the house but her wish was ignored. When the noises became unbearable, Anne's coffin was opened and it was found that the head was already severed from the body. The skull was taken to the hall and the noises stopped!

Haunted Island Britain has more ghosts per square mile than anywhere else in the world!

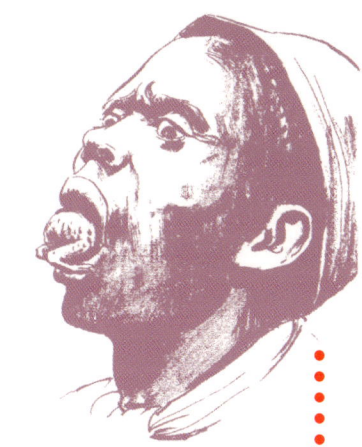

A native, accused of witchcraft in Kenya, Africa, was forced to hold a live frog in his mouth. If it slid down his throat, he was guilty. If not, he was innocent.

Fading Husband Seven people saw Captain Towns in his home near Sydney, Australia, in May 1873. However, the Captain had died six weeks before. When Mrs. Towns approached the apparition, it vanished and was never seen again.

Well-dressed Ghost The ghost of an 18th-century dandy seen by the author Baroness Orczy on a London Underground station, inspired her to write her stories about the Scarlet Pimpernel.

FIT TO BE WITCHES
In December 1691, seven young girls of Salem, Massachusetts, were thrown into violent fits when they played with an "oracle." Later they began seeing "spectral figures" that hit and scratched them. The girls blamed three local women for their ills and this started off the most famous witch hunt trial in American history.

Aleister Crowley was dubbed "The World's Wickedest Man" because he claimed he had sold his soul to the Devil. Crowley liked to be known as "The Beast of the Apocalypse" and admitted to taking part in occult rituals and studying the secret powers of nature.

Magic in a Box

David Blaine from New York has become something of a modern-day phenomenon as an illusionist and close-up magician.

He first gained acclaim when he roamed the streets of various cities in the U.S.A., performing amazing, televised, close-up magic for random individuals. He has since attempted and succeeded in such endeavors as standing in a block of ice for hours on end, being suspended in a box, and being buried alive for one week. However, his phenomenal skills as a magician have led people to believe that these feats are purely illusionary!

In November 2000, David Blaine stood in the middle of Times Square, New York, surrounded by a 6-ton block of ice! He stood for more than 60 hours while spectators wandered round the ice, peering in at him. He emerged with swollen legs, but otherwise physically unharmed.

Street Magic
David Blaine has astounded people all over the world with his street magic. He was seen pulling the head off a chicken before putting it back on, causing no apparent harm to the creature. During one trick he appeared to reach through ordinary glass to pull out a watch from a jewelry store display, and he once pulled a piece of string from his stomach!

In 2002, David Blaine stood on the 80-ft (24-m) pole in Bryant Park, New York City, for 35 hours straight! After being subjected to the wind, darkness of night, and the constant stares of the crowd from the ground below, he jumped into a pile of cardboard boxes that had been set up by his team beneath the pole.

Beyond Understanding

"Living on only water and under constant observation for 44 days straight"

Doctor, Doctor At 16 years old, David Blaine levitated in front of his doctor, who took him in for immediate examination!

Magical Code Mysterious Stranger, David Blaine's book, is said to contain a code that, if read properly, can lead to hidden treasure!

Harry Houdini's original idea was the inspiration for David Blaine's New York feat in 1999. Blaine was lowered into the ground and buried alive in a glass box for one week, living on only four tablespoons of water a day.

Noah Kelly from England mimicked David Blaine's ice feat by covering himself in blocks of cheese in a shopping center in Weston-Super-Mare, England, for 48 hours!

David Blaine carried out another punishing feat of endurance in October 2003, when he spent 44 days in a glass box suspended from Tower Bridge, London, England. He was only allowed water during his time in the box, and was under constant observation from large crowds on the ground below. When he emerged from the box after 44 days, he had lost almost 55 lb (25 kg), and over the following weeks, was taken through a refeeding program in order to regain his health.

The Street of the Seven Devils in Jever, Germany, is so named because three men and four women living on it were executed for sorcery.

Suspended in Air In 1936, Subbayah Pullavar of India, levitated in front of 150 onlookers! Pullavar started by pouring water around a tent, which he then entered, hidden from the audience for several minutes. When the tent was removed, the audience were shocked to see him apparently in a trance and suspended horizontally about 3 ft (1 m) in the air. Some of the audience members waved objects underneath him but could find no evidence of support. Once the tent was placed around him again, he was seen by some onlookers descending back down to the ground, still horizontal!

Magical Name Welsh magician Richard Valentine Pitchford was a failure as "Valentine Professor Thomas" and "Val Raymond" but a huge success when billed as "Cardini"!

Devil Neighbor Near the Vatican in Rome, there is a museum devoted entirely to the Devil.

Walking Through Walls In 1986, American magician David Copperfield caused a sensation when, on a televised show, he walked through the solid mass of the Great Wall of China. However, his feat was not the first such event, as the English magician P.T. Selbit walked through a brick wall on stage back in 1914.

Witch's Craft Witches were once thought to be able to sail about in empty eggshells, which is probably why even today people often smash the shells after eating an egg.

This severed head may look very convincing, but is actually an illusion! It is created by vertically standing two mirrors under the table where the person's head is resting.

At the End of His Rope
In the Indian Rope Trick a *jaduwallah* (magician) throws a rope into the air, where it remains suspended. A small boy climbs up the rope and disappears. The magician orders the boy to descend and, receiving no response, climbs up the rope with a dagger between his teeth. He, too, vanishes! Loud screams are heard from the heavens and the dismembered body of the boy falls to the ground bit by bit. The magician reappears, shins down the rope, which then falls limp to the ground. The bits of the boy are gathered into a large sack and the boy emerges from the sack fully restored and none the worse for his dreadful experience. It is one of the most amazing feats in magic but very few people know how it is done!

Karachi and his son Khydar demonstrated their version of the Indian Rope Trick in 1935.

Beyond Understanding

Light Touch In 1995, a woman on the Isle of Wight, Britain, complained that a ghost had switched on the electrical appliances in her holiday cottage! The electricity board said it was the first time a high bill had been blamed on a ghost!

Patience of a Saint St. Kevin, a 6th-century Irish saint, was canonized for tolerating the ghost of a woman he had murdered!

Burning Stakes Between 1621 and 1640, 30,000 women were accused of witchcraft and burned at the stake.

No Comforter Mrs. Dora Monroe moved into a house in Wisconsin in 1972 and found a haunted quilt! People who slept under it said that it talked to them, tugged itself off the bed, and even crawled under furniture!

GHOST TOWN, U.K.

The village of Pluckley is reputed to be the most haunted village in Britain. It has at least 11 ghosts:

- The 12th-century Lady Dering haunts the graveyard
- A screaming worker who was smothered by clay that fell from a container at a brickworks
- A highwayman who was attacked and speared to a tree at Fright Corner
- A mysterious lady in white
- A ghostly monk who haunts the grounds of a house
- A phantom coach drawn by four ghostly horses
- The black ghost of the old ruined mill
- A gypsy woman who was burned to death
- A lady who killed herself by drinking the juice of poisonous berries
- A schoolmaster who hanged himself in the village
- A colonel who hanged himself in the woods

Eddie Coxon took this photograph during a flower festival in a church in Staffordshire, England. He was sure that no one was in front of the camera, yet this ghostly figure appears in the photograph!

> **"Man's figure appears in 'empty church' photograph"**

Lesson in History Coleen Butterbaugh in October 1963 in a room at Nebraska Wesleyan University, saw a woman vanish! When she described the incident to officials, she was shown a photo of the lady she had seen—Clarissa Mills, who had died in that room in 1936.

LINCOLN STALKS THE WHITE HOUSE

When Franklin D. Roosevelt was president, Queen Wilhelmina of the Netherlands reported seeing the ghost of Abraham Lincoln in the White House. President Theodore Roosevelt, Lady Bird Johnson, President Harry S Truman, and President Dwight Eisenhower also claimed to have seen this ghost.

Grave-robbers' Curse

The archeologists who were present when the inner chamber of Tutankhamun's tomb was opened for the first time in 3,000 years, on February 17, 1923, ignored the warning inscribed above the tomb entrance to warn off intruders:

"*Death will come to those who disturb the sleep of the pharaohs*"

Howard Carter and his team of archeologists opened Tutankhamun's tomb in Egypt in 1922, oblivious to the death warning inscribed above the tomb's entrance.

PREDICTIONS OF NOSTRADAMUS

- The Parliament of London will put their king to death—Charles I was executed in London in 1649
- London to be burned by fire in three times twenty plus six—Great Fire of London 1666
- An emperor will be born near Italy and for 14 years he will hold the tyranny—Napoleon was born in Corsica, an island near Italy, and was in power from 1799 to 1814
- The dreadful war is prepared in the West, the following year the pestilence will come—World War I was followed by worldwide influenza
- For not wanting to consent to divorce the king of the islands will be forced to flee—King Edward VIII was forced to abdicate when he insisted on marrying the divorced Mrs. Simpson

Lord Carnarvon, the sponsor of the expedition, died 47 days after entering the tomb and various other expedition members died shortly after their return to England. Six years later, 12 of the expedition members were dead, and after a further seven years, only two of the excavators survived. From the original team, only Howard Carter lived into old age.

Novel Story When actor Antony Hopkins was offered the leading role in the 1974 movie *The Girl from Petrovka*, he searched in vain for a copy of the George Feifer novel on which the movie was based. While waiting for his train home he spotted a book lying on a bench. It was a copy of *The Girl from Petrovka*. During the filming in Vienna the actor was introduced to the novelist. It transpired that Feifer had lent his personal copy to a friend who had lost it in London. Hopkins showed Feifer the book he had found. It was Feifer's own copy!

A NUMBER OF PROBABILITIES

Did you know that in any group of 23 people, there is about a 50 percent chance that two of them will share the same birthday? It's nothing at all to do with coincidence, but everything to do with statistics.

Beyond Understanding

PLUM OCCASIONS
The French poet Emile Deschamps once shared a table with a Monsieur de Fortgibu who was fond of plum pudding, and persuaded the poet to try some. Years later, Deschamps saw a plum pudding in a restaurant and requested a slice but was told it was reserved for another customer. This was his old friend Monsieur de Fortgibu! Several years after, Descamps attended a dinner party where one of the dishes was plum pudding. He told the story of the strange coincidence and everyone joked that Fortgibu might arrive. And he did. He had been invited to a dinner nearby but had got lost! "Three times in my life I have eaten plum pudding," said Deschamps "And three times have I seen Monsieur de Fortgibu."

Words out of Place Just prior to the Normandy landings of World War II, crosswords in the English newspaper *The Daily Telegraph* included the answers Omaha, Utah, Mulberry, and Neptune. They were all secret code names for the landings. The answer to another clue was Overlord, the code name for the operation itself. The crossword compiler, schoolteacher Leonard Dawe, was very quickly investigated by intelligence officers, but it turned out to be an astonishing coincidence.

Fall Guy Joseph Figlock was walking past a 14-story building in Detroit in 1975, when a baby fell from the building and landed on him. A year later another baby fell from the same building and survived the drop by falling on—Joseph Figlock!

Room Service In 1953 American journalist Irving Kupcinet traveled to Britain from Paris. In his hotel room he found some personal belongings of his friend, basketball player Harry Hannin. Two days later Kupcinet received a letter from Hannin in Paris, which said: "You'll never believe this, but I've just found a tie with your name on it in my hotel room."

Cradle to the Altar Alan Redgrave and Melanie Somerville had an instant rapport when they first met in a supermarket. They soon discovered that they had both been born on the same day, in the same hospital, and that their cots were placed together in the ward. Alan and Melanie married one another in 2003.

Bee Congregation Mrs. Margaret Bell, a well-known beekeeper in the English town of Ludlow, died in June 1994. For an hour during Mrs. Bell's funeral a swarm of bees settled on a building in Bell Lane!

An astrologer once assured William the Conqueror that he would invade England with 900 ships and in that vast armada, only one man would die. Only one man failed to survive the voyage—the astrologer!

Hanging Together Three men were hanged in London for murdering a man at a place called Greenberry Hill. The surnames of the murderers were Green, Berry, and Hill!

David Mandell claims to have had premonitions in his dreams, which he sketched afterwards. He is seen here with some of the drawings, which bear a striking resemblance to events that happened shortly after his dreams.

Copper-plated Katie

A psychic, named Katie, displayed the ability to grow copper on her skin! Katie had various psychic abilities, such as the ability to levitate objects, bend metal, and write medieval French while in a trance.

Psychic researcher Dr. Berthold E. Schwarz from Florida, studied Katie for some time and would watch her during her trances, as the copper appeared. It was also discovered that copper could be grown on objects that she carried, or people whom she touched. The copper was examined and found to contain 98 percent copper traces and two percent zinc. Examinations carried out on Katie led people to believe that she was exhibiting psychic side-effects, similar to the ectoplasm that mediums are said to be able to create from their mouths during states of trance.

Before she entered a trance, Dr. Schwarz would examine Katie closely and find no traces of copper, but it would often appear on her face, neck, hands, and back shortly after entering the trance. Peeling away the copper would often cause Katie some discomfort.

TELEPATHIC ESCAPE

In 1942, telepathy saved the life of British prime minister Sir Winston Churchill. He was scheduled to attend a military exercise on April 13, but, after a premonition, decided not to go. During the exercise 27 people were accidentally shot dead and 68 were seriously wounded. Brigadier Grant Taylor, who stood in for Churchill on that fateful day, was killed. Had Churchill attended as originally planned, the entire course of British history might have changed.

College Test The first scientific examination of ESP was undertaken by Professor Rhine at Duke University, North Carolina. Over 40 years, numerous people were tested and Rhine came to the conclusion that extra sensory perception or some form of telepathic communication does exist.

Water Diviner In 1952 Colonel Harry Grattan of the Royal Engineers was employed by the British Army to locate water sources in Germany. As a dowser (water locater) with years of experience, he successfully located many sites that produced water.

Swinging for Oil Ace Gotowski was called upon by the Fox Brewing Company of Chicago to search for oil in 1943. Using a pendulum Gotowski identified a suitable site; when the company drilled where he had indicated, it was discovered that he had located the largest oil field at that time.

Beyond Understanding

It would appear that some people have magnetic abilities. In 1994, Edward Naumov from Moscow, Russia, displayed his ability to pin metal objects to someone. The subject found that no matter how hard he tried to resist the objects, Naumov's "energy" pinned them to him with no signs of touching or trickery!

Reading on the Radio Sydney and Lesley Piddington baffled British radio listeners with their thought-reading feats in 1949. They claim to have sent messages from the BBC to an underwater diving bell, using telepathy.

Long Distance Telepathy As part of a number of scientific tests in Russia in 1966, Karl Nikolatev was handed a sealed package chosen at random from a series of identical boxes. Nikolatev's friend, Yuri Kamensky, was 1,800 mi (2,900 km) away. While Nikolatev opened the box, Kamensky described the contents accurately. Both men were supervised by scientific teams to ensure that there was no trickery.

Safe Return In 1960 the daughter of an American professor had went missing. After two months, in desperation the professor telephoned the Dutch clairvoyant Gerard Croiset, who was famous for helping in several police cases. Croiset told the father that he would hear from his daughter in six days. Six days later the professor went downstairs for breakfast and found his daughter sitting in the living room, completely safe!

Tragedy Foreseen On October 20, 1966, a woman in Plymouth, England, told people in her church congregation that she had received a vision of an avalanche of coal in South Wales. The following day a mass of coal slid down from a coal tip onto the Welsh village of Aberfan, killing over 100 children and many adults.

Mental Moves Nelya Mikhaileva moved objects with her mind! In 1968 Russian scientists filmed her as she made a piece of bread and a glass tumbler move, and stopped and started a clock pendulum without touching anything.

Uri Geller, the Israeli psychic, explained his power to bend keys at a distance while taking part in a British radio call-in program in 1973. Minutes later the switchboard was lit up with calls reporting that keys, forks, spoons, and nails had bent spontaneously, and that watches and clocks that had not run for years had started to work again.

Putting Feet to the Fire

As part of their religious practices, people in Fiji, Asia, and India walk through red-hot coals without any apparent injury. In Fiji, the ceremony once held for religious reasons, is performed regularly for tourists. In India and other parts of Asia, the ceremony is still performed for religious reasons, and participants are required to prepare themselves spiritually before the ceremony. Many western people have tried fire walking without problems, even though the coals are hot enough to cause wood to burst into flame immediately. The ability to avoid injury seems to be because people walk on hot ashes, not on the flaming coals or wood, and because the heat vaporizes water in the skin and produces a protective film.

Fire walking is a feature at the annual Vegetarian Festival in Phuket, southern Thailand. The Buddhist devotees perform rituals to evoke good luck and purge their bodies of any evil.

Bursting into Flames

The charred remains of Dr. Bentley of Coudersport, Pennsylvania, baffled those who found him in his bathroom on December 5, 1966.

There have been many reports of people bursting into flames (spontaneous human combustion), and it is a phenomenon for which there appears to be no logical explanation. Frequently, the body is found partly consumed in a sealed room that is filled with soot and greasy particles. A common feature is that only part of the body is consumed and often combustible material nearby is completely unharmed. It was once believed that spontaneous combustion was a highly extreme reaction to drinking too much brandy or being too angry! What is most baffling is that even in a crematorium, where temperatures can reach up to 1,800°F (1,000°C), bones are not completely burned as they can be in cases of spontaneous combustion.

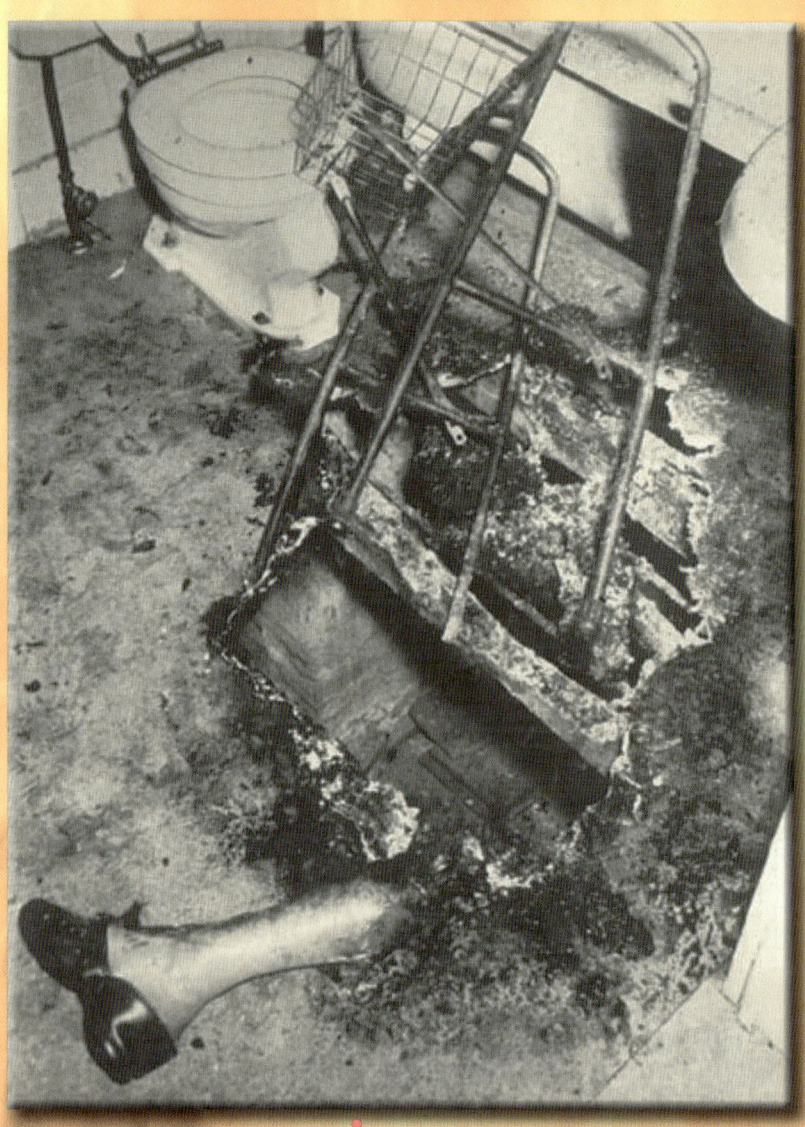

GONE IN A FLASH

- **Mrs. Mary Reezer—Florida, 1951.** The wall behind her chair and a pile of newspapers nearby had not been burned
- **Billy Peterson—Detroit, 1959.** The heat inside the car was so great that part of the dashboard melted, but Billy's clothes were unharmed!
- **Paul Hayes—London, 1985.** A fire engulfed him as he was walking in Stepney Green. The flames disappeared just as suddenly

Shocked Audience In 1880 an eminent physician, Dr. B.H. Hartwell, and several other people witnessed the death of a woman in Massachusetts, who burst into flames.

Closed in a Car In 1988, in Sydney, Australia, an elderly lady was sitting in a parked car. Minutes later, people noticed smoke coming from the vehicle, followed by an explosion. The victim was pulled out alive, but died a week later. Investigators found no trace of gas, electrical problems, or wiring faults—the case remains a mystery.

A pile of ashes and half a leg were all that was left of Dr. Bentley. An intense heat had consumed his body, but apart from the burned-through hole in the floor, little else had been damaged.

Barn Untouched In 1888 the body of an old laborer was found in a hayloft in Aberdeen, Scotland. He had burned to death but his face showed no signs of pain. The beam on which he was lying was unharmed, and nearby bales of hay had not burned.

Beyond Understanding

Clue to the Triangle?
The sea between Bermuda, Florida, and Puerto Rico is reputed to have secret powers that have caused the disappearance of numerous ships and aircraft. Stories about the Bermuda Triangle began when five Avenger bombers vanished within five hours of taking off from Fort Lauderdale Naval Air Station on December 5, 1945. An interesting possible explanation was found in 2000, when a 72-ft (22-m) steel-hulled fishing trawler was found resting almost undamaged in a large crater on the bed of the North Sea, 93 mi (150 km) east of Scotland. The crater could have been caused by the release of a huge bubble of methane gas. Investigation found that the seabed in this area contained large deposits of an ice-like substance called methane hydrate, which is capable of suddenly releasing huge amounts of methane gas, which could have created a huge gas bubble to rise to the surface, causing a large ship to sink suddenly. This could also be the explanation for such disappearances in the Bermuda Triangle.

MISSING CRAFT
- *Bomber flight 19*—1945
- *Martin Mariner*—1945
- *City Belle*—1946
- *Superfortress*—1947
- *DC-3*—1948
- *Star Ariel*—1949
- *Revonoc*—1958
- *Witchcraft*—1967

Ghost on Ice While crossing a frozen lake in Canada, explorer James Alan Rennie saw tracks being formed in the ice with no visible explanation. As the tracks approached "I stood stock still, filled with reasonless panic. The tracks came within 50 yd [45 m] of me, then 20, then ten—then smack!
I shouted as a large blob of water hit me in the face. I swung round, brushing the water from my eyes, and saw the tracks continuing across the lake."

Wounded In September 1983, an Argentinean housewife had a vision of the Virgin Mary, and heard the first of 1,800 religious messages. A year later, mysterious red sores broke out on her wrists, feet, and forehead, representing the wounds suffered by Christ in his crucifixion.

Stigmata have appeared over the centuries on many highly religious people, and are often associated with "miracle cures." Italian Giorgio Bongiovanni is an unusual stigmatic in that he is not a religious person, yet he claims that in 1989 the Blessed Virgin Mary came to him in a vision and told him to travel to Fatima, Portugal. Six months after he did so, he received the first signs of the stigmata, the wounds in the palms of his hands. Since, he has also received wounds in his feet, side, and forehead. These wounds bleed daily and doctors can find no explanation for them.

Water Finders Many people seem to possess a mysterious ability to find hidden water. The dowser (person who locates water underground) holds a Y-shaped twig, traditionally of hazel, which moves violently when underground water is located. Mineral deposits and even underground cables have been located using this and similar methods, but no one seems to know exactly how or why it works.

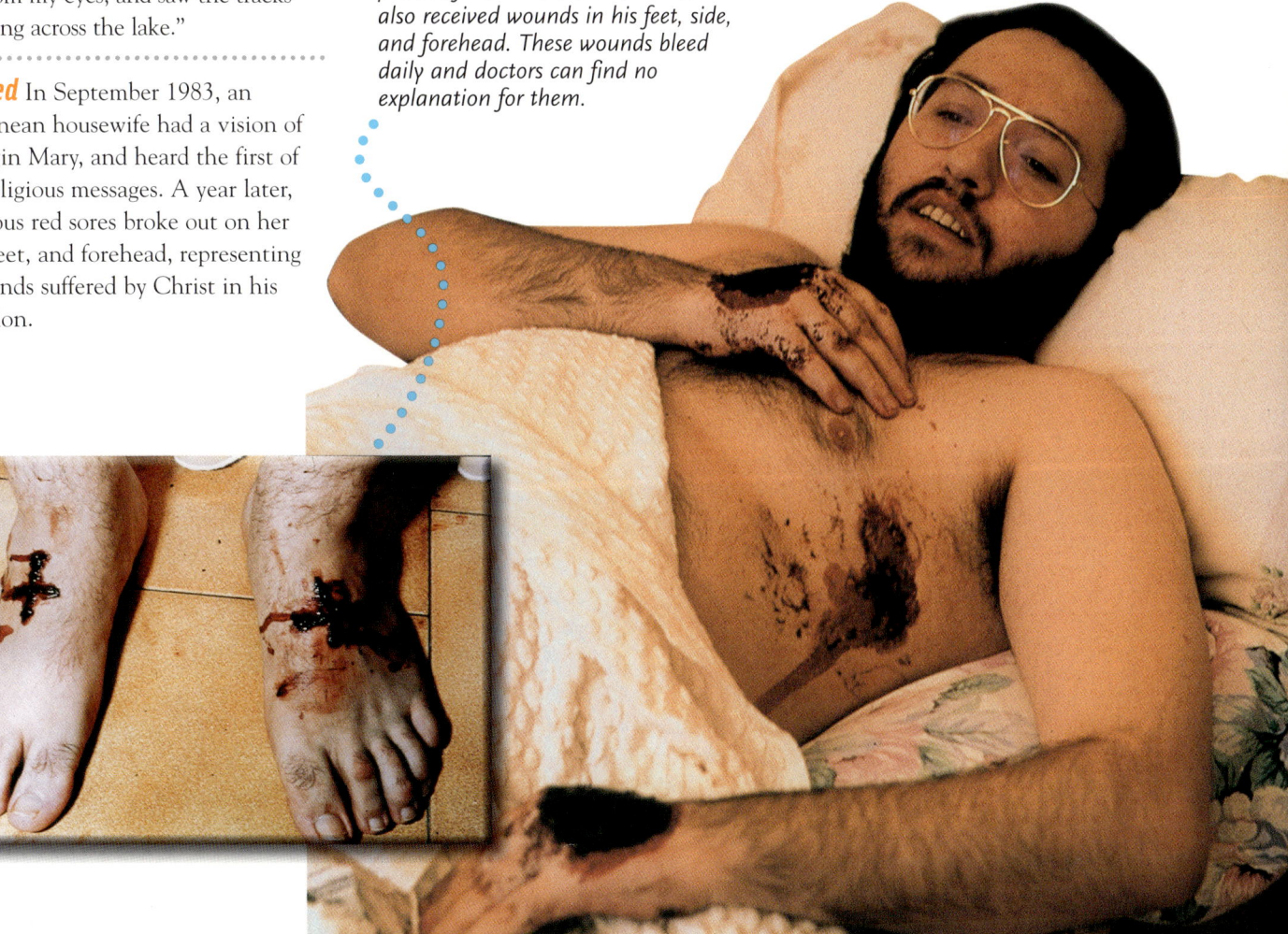

GLOBSTER INVASION
In 1960, two Australian ranch hands found a gigantic carcass washed up on a remote beach in Tasmania. It was more than 20 ft (6 m) long, and 18 ft (5.5 m) wide. It was shaped like a turtle, and covered by greasy hair. Dubbed a "globster," a larger, similar creature was found in New Zealand in 1965, and another in Tasmania in 1970. Some have identified these creatures as blubber from dead whales, while others say they remain a mystery.

Fishy Rain Bass and shad fell to the ground in Marksville, Louisiana, on October 23, 1947. A shower of small fish, including smelts and flounder, fell from the skies in the garden of Ron Langton in West Ham, London, on May 27, 1984. The following year, a shower of fish fell in the backyard of Louis Castoreno in Fort Worth, Texas, on May 8, 1985.

Flop Jelly Rowland Moody of Southampton, England, was in his conservatory during a heavy snowstorm on February 12, 1979, when he heard something hit the roof of his house and bounce down to the ground. When he went outside to investigate, he found that his garden and those of his neighbors were covered with cress seeds (plant eaten in salads) coated in a sticky jelly.

On a dried-up lake in Death Valley, California, can be found the moving stones! These stones travel large distances, creating a variety of tracks, from straight, to curved or zig-zagged, without any apparent help. Some geologists attribute the phenomenon to strong winds, but others believe that there are stranger forces at work!

Ring of Misfortune Silent movie star Rudolph Valentino bought a ring that was supposed to be unlucky. When he wore it, his movies were flops. Several people who obtained the ring after Valentino's death fell ill or were killed.

Signs in the Cornfields
Mysterious, huge patterns in standing corn, sometimes hundreds of feet across, began appearing in the 1970s in southern England. They consisted of huge circles where the corn had been pressed down, with all the stems facing in the same direction. Soon the crop circle designs became more elaborate, and spread to other parts of the world. Were they messages from aliens, or were they caused by some mysterious "ion plasma vortices"—a new scientific term invented by the self-styled cereologists who studied the phenomenon? Or are they just a new form of graffiti art carried out by hoaxers?

The Hopi Indians of Arizona believed that crop circles were signs that the world would soon end.

"Messages from aliens"

CROP SHOCKS
- Crop circles were reported as early as AD 815 in Lyon, France
- In the 16th century, a woodcut illustration shows the devil mowing patterns in a field
- More than 5,000 cases have been reported over the past 20 years
- Markings were once found in the snow in Afghanistan at an altitude of 20,000 ft (6,100 m)
- A pattern was once found underwater in a paddy field in Japan

Beyond Understanding

Beasts Stalk England

One morning in 1994, actress Sarah Miles saw something unusual near her house in West Sussex. It was a huge, black cat, as big as a mastiff, and mysterious in appearance! From this sighting grew the legend of the Beast of Bodmin Moor.

Since the 1960s, there have been similar reports of large cats prowling the wild parts of Britain, and sometimes straying into built-up areas. Searches have failed to reveal them, though photographs have been taken, and livestock has been found that appears to have been killed by a large animal. However, some wild cats have been shot by farmers or run over, and among the corpses have been pumas and lynxes, as well as smaller types of jungle cat, which have been subsequently been blamed for the attacks.

This mould was made to show the size of a paw print that was discovered in West Sussex, England, said to be similar to the legendary Beast of Bodmin Moor.

This image was caught on camera by Rosie Rhodes in 1995, and is believed to be the Beast of Bodmin Moor. It was apparently far too large to be a domestic animal.

MYSTERY CREATURES

- Almas—Russia
- Orang Pendek—Sumatra
- Sasquatch—North America
- Wild Man of Hubei—southern China
- Yeti—Himalayas
- Yowie—Australia

The Tracks of Bigfoot

There have been many reported sightings of a large, hairy, man-like creature—the Sasquatch—in Canada and the United States. The Sasquatch is popularly known as Bigfoot because most of the evidence of its existence is in the form of large footprints. The most impressive of these were found at Bossburgh, Washington State, in October 1969. Each footprint measured about 18 in (46 cm) long and the tracks covered about 0.5 mi (0.8 km).

A Forest Patrol officer took this photograph of "Bigfoot" in 1995, near Mount Rainier in Washington State. However, many believe it is a hoax photograph.

Ripley's YETI FOOTPRINT EXHIBIT NO: 22449 — NEGATIVE CASTING OF A YETI FOOTPRINT, CREATED IN TIBET IN THE 1950s

Solid Curse A stone in the American city of Augusta, Georgia, was the cause of many deaths. It originally stood in the old slave market and rebellious slaves were tied to it and flogged. A curse was placed on the stone by the mother of a man who was killed by such a flogging. It is said that the stone has been the cause of numerous deaths every time someone has tried to move it.

Lost Civilization Atlantis, according to the Greek philosopher Plato, was an island civilization destroyed by earthquakes and swallowed up by the sea. Many attempts have been made to discover the location of this island, but without success.

LAKE MONSTERS

- Lake Champlain, U.S.A. (Champ)
- Lake Chini, Malaysia
- Lake Khaiyr, Russia
- Lake Nahuel Huapi, Argentina
- Lake Okanagan, Canada
- Loch Ness, Scotland (Nessie)
- Lough Rea, Ireland
- Tianchitianchi Lake, China

Deadly Gold No one who has seen the Lost Dutchman Mine of Superstition Mountain in Arizona has lived to tell the tale. According to local legend the mine is overflowing with gold, but every man who found it was killed by Apache Indians who were angry at the desecration of their land.

Flying Dutchman Stories of phantom ships abound, but the most famous is of the *Flying Dutchman*, which is condemned to sail around the Cape of Good Hope forever.

Snuff of That! Gold prospector Albert Ostmann was kidnapped by a family of Sasquatch in 1924 and only escaped when the male became ill after eating a box of snuff!

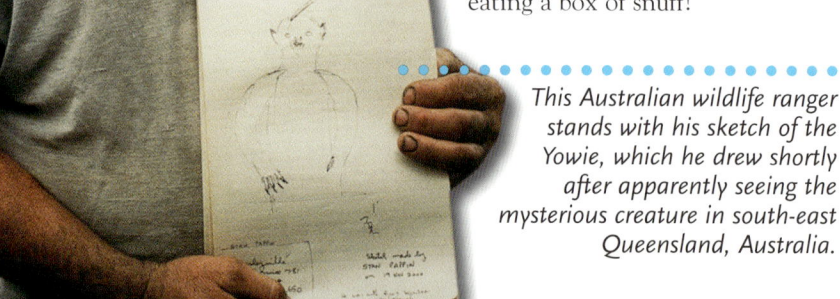

This Australian wildlife ranger stands with his sketch of the Yowie, which he drew shortly after apparently seeing the mysterious creature in south-east Queensland, Australia.

Beyond Understanding 31

Atlantis West The Pacific Ocean version of Atlantis is the Great Empire of Mu. It was believed that Mu was the cradle of civilization, which sank beneath the waters of the Pacific over 12,000 years ago. No one knows its location.

Ripley's CHUPACABRA FOOTPRINT
EXHIBIT NO: 22451
POSITIVE CASTING OF A CHUPACABRA FOOTPRINT, CREATED IN PUERTO RICO IN THE LATE 1990s

In 1995 in Puerto Rico, a strange creature was accused of attacking domestic animals and draining their blood through a single puncture wound. Eye-witnesses said that it resembled a kangaroo, with sharp fangs, red, lidless eyes, and bat wings, with spikes running down its back. The locals called the creature El Chupacabras, which means "goatsucker."

This kitten, found in Manchester, England, had a broad flat tail and "wings." The 11 in (28 cm) "wings" grew from the shoulder bone.

Vanishing Colony When John White returned from England to the island of Roanoke in Virginia, all the colonists he had left four years earlier had disappeared without a trace. No one knows what fate befell them.

Fatal Tune The song "Gloomy Sunday" was banned by Britain's BBC because it has caused too many deaths. Written in 1935 by Lazzlo Javor, a Hungarian poet, the song was associated with over 200 deaths around the world.

Path to Atlantis? American psychic Edgar Cayce predicted that remains of the temples of Atlantis would be discovered in the sea near the island of Bimini in the Bahamas in 1968 or 1969. A long "pavement" of symmetrically shaped stones was discovered on the seabed there in 1968!

Nessie's Getting Old Sightings of the creature said to inhabit Loch Ness in Scotland have been reported regularly since the 6th century. In modern times, photographs have been taken purporting to show the monster but, so far, in spite of repeated scientific expeditions, no physical evidence has been found.

LEAPING LEGEND
Victorian England was terrorized by a creature that attacked people, jumped over houses, and was impervious to bullets! Wearing a metallic-like suit and a glass and metal helmet, with talons projecting from its sleeves, it was nicknamed Spring-Heeled Jack because of its remarkable ability to jump over houses. For a period of 66 years from 1838, Jack spread panic throughout the land. But after a spectacular appearance in Liverpool in 1904 he was never seen again—and to this day no one knows who, or what, it was.

Ghostly Drumbeat A drum owned by Sir Francis Drake, England's heroic 16th-century admiral, is reported to have sounded without human hands to mark the outbreak of World War I.

Allegedly this is the hand of a yeti discovered at an altitude of 20,000 ft (6,100 m) in the Himalayas, on the border between Tibet and Nepal. In 1951, Eric Shipton photographed a long trail of huge man-like footprints. Two years later, Sir Edmund Hillary saw similar tracks during the first ascent of Mount Everest. They were believed to be the tracks of the Yeti or Abominable Snowman. The creature seems to exist, but no one knows what it is. Some people think that it is a bear, or an unknown great ape, or even a primitive form of human.

Haunting Puzzle

Sarah Winchester, of California, designed what may be the most puzzling house ever—and then spent 38 years trying to build it.

Doors that open onto blank walls, stairs that lead nowhere, trapdoors beneath which there are no openings, and balconies with no entrances are just some of the fascinating features Sarah built into her strange house in San Jose in Santa Clara Valley, California. From 1884 to 1922, builders and carpenters were kept busy building every day until Sarah died. During her life, Mrs. Winchester allowed no one inside the house except the workmen and a few maids. Today it is believed that the Winchester Mystery House is haunted by the ghosts of Sarah's husband and daughter.

WINCHESTER HOUSE

- 950 doors—excluding cabinet doors, some of which lead nowhere
- 10,000 windows—most of which have 13 panes
- 47 fireplaces—many have flues that lead nowhere
- 17 chimneys—at present, with evidence of two others
- 160 rooms—in total
- 5 kitchens—possibly 6
- 40 bedrooms—possibly more
- 13 bathrooms
- 2 ballrooms—unfinished
- 40 staircases—some of which seem to go nowhere
- 52 skylights—many of which appear not to let in any light
- 7 stories—prior to the 1906 earthquake, now 4

Among the many strange and fascinating features of the house are a number of staircases that lead nowhere.

Built in San Jose, California, Sarah Winchester's house was originally built seven stories high! It was reduced to four stories in 1906, after damage caused by the famous San Francisco earthquake.

Beyond Understanding

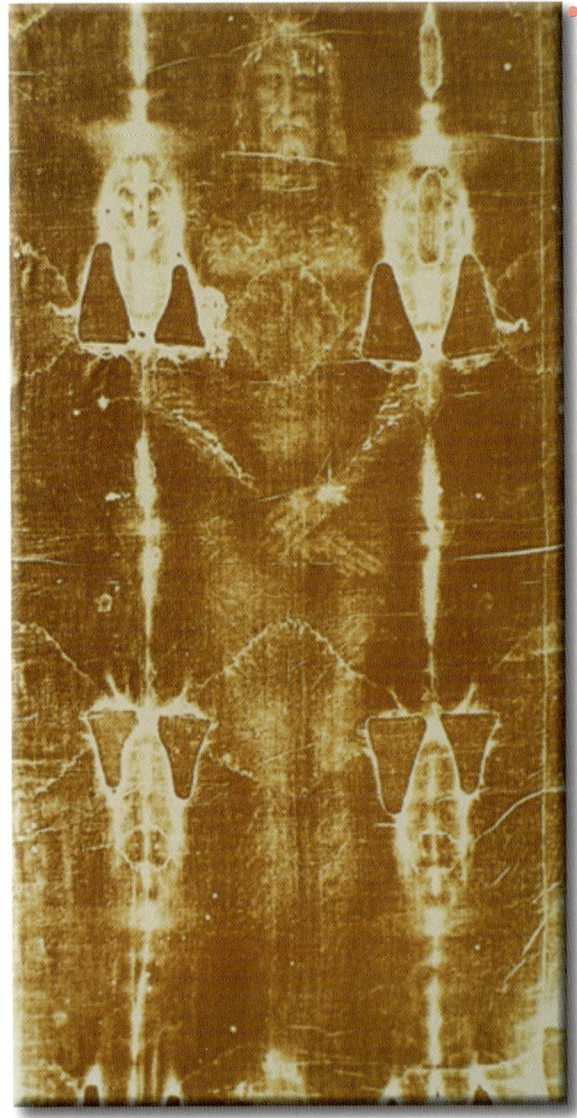

Despite attempts to prove the date of origin of the Turin Shroud by analysis, such as carbon dating, the shroud remains a mystery. Many believe that it is the shroud that Christ was covered with at his burial, while others believe it is a medieval forgery.

OPTICAL ILLUSION — IS IT A DUCK OR A RABBIT?

To see the duck, you need to rotate the image counter-clockwise. To see the rabbit, look at it from the right.

Men They Couldn't Hang No matter how hard prison authorities tried, they could not hang John Lee. In 1885, 19-year-old Lee was sentenced to death for killing his employer. Several unsuccessful attempts were made to hang him and he was eventually reprieved.

Chaos in the Crypt Coffins were thrown around a family vault in Bridgetown, Barbados, even though the vault was sealed! Over the next eight years, every time the vault was reopened to inter a family member, the coffins had been disturbed—but there was no sign of entry to the tomb!

Priest Preserved When the body of Reverend Father Paul of Moll was exhumed on July 24, 1899, it was found to be perfectly preserved. The Belgian priest had died three years previously.

Body Survives In 1921, when the body of Julia Buccola Petta was exhumed seven years after her death during childbirth, her body was found to be in perfect condition.

Mountaintop Theater There are over 200 stone blocks grouped to form what appears to be an amphitheater on the 2-mi (3-km) long plateau of El Enladrillado, in Chile. Archeologists do not know what the site is for, who prepared the giant blocks, or how they were transported to the site, which can only be reached by a three-hour journey on horseback.

Which is greater? The height of the hat or the width of the brim?

Neither! They are both the same size.

The plain of Nazca, Peru, is covered with strange lines, some of which form patterns and others the shapes of animals. They can only be seen properly from the air—but the Inca people who made them had no knowledge of flight.

Index

A
abductees 11
Aberfan tragedy 25
"abracadabra" 16
Adamski, George 11
age of the universe 8
Aldrin, Edwin "Buzz" 7
aliens 11–14
   abductees 11
   alien discoveries 12, 14
   group sighting 12
   invasion panic 11
   letter B on Mars 12
   Martian language 11
   waving aliens 14
   see also UFOs
Allingham, Cedric 14
Alminant Saldanha 12
America, eclipse and the discovery of 10
America's first manned space flight 10
American Spiritualist movement, origin of 16
American/Russian meeting in space 10
Apollo spaceships 7, 10
Area 51, Nevada 14
Armstrong, Neil 7
Arnold, Kenneth 13
Atlantis 30, 31

B
Barringer crater, Arizona 8
Beast of Bodmin Moor 29
Bell, Mrs. Margaret 23
Bellonzo 13
Bentley, Dr. 26
Bermuda Triangle 27
Bigfoot 30
Blaine, David 18–19
Bongiovanni, Giorgio 27
Brahe, Tycho 8
Bull, Henry 16
burns from UFO 13
Burton Agnes Hall, Bridlington, England 17
Butterbaugh, Coleen 21

C
Carnarvon, Lord 22
Carter, Howard 22
Castoreno, Louis 27
Cayce, Edgar 31
Charles I 22
Chinese moon landing, early 7
chupacabra footprint 31
Churchill, Sir Winston 24
coincidences see prophecies and coincidences
Columbus, Christopher 10, 13
combustion, spontaneous human 26
comets 9
Copperfield, David 20
Coxon, Eddie 21
craft, missing 27
crater, largest meteorite 8
creatures, mystery 29
Croiset, Gerard 25
crop circles 28
Crowley, Aleister 17
Curran, Mrs. John 16
cursed stone 30

D
Dawe, Leonard 23
de Fortgibu, Monsieur 23
Death Valley, California 28
Democritus of Addesa 9
Deschamps, Emile 23
discoveries, alien 12, 14
Douglas Home, Daniel 16
Drake, Sir Francis 31

E
earth 6, 8, 9
   measurements 9
eclipse and the discovery of America 10
Edward VIII 22
Eisenhower, Dwight 21
El Enladrillado, Chile 33
Endurance TV game show 19
Eratosthenes of Cyrene 9
extra sensory perception 24–25
eye, trick of the 33

F
Farlow, Carl 12
Feifer, George 22
Figlock, Joseph 23
fire walking 25
first manned space flight 9
fish, in space 9
flight, America's first manned space 10
flying discs, Nazi 13
Flying Dutchman 30
flying saucer experiment 12
"flying saucer," origin of 13
footprint, chupacabra 31
fortune telling 17
Fox Brewing Company, Chicago 24
Fox, Kate and Margaretta 16
Freedom 7 spacecraft 10

G
Gagarin, Yuri 9, 10
Geller, Uri 25
ghostly photographs 16, 21
Gill, Father 14
Girl from Petrovka, The 22
Gloomy Sunday 31
Gotowski, Ace 24
Grattan, Harry 24
gravity 6, 9
Great Fire of London 22
Griffith, Anne 17

H
Habermohl 13
"Happy Birthday" in space 10
Harden, Tomas 15
Harper, Peggy 15
Hartwell, Dr. B.H. 26
hauntings, most haunted village 21
Hayes, Paul 26
head, severed 20
Hemingway, Ernest 16
Hill, Betty and Barney 11
Hillary, Sir Edmund 31
Hopi Indians, Arizona 28
Hopkins, Antony 22
Houdini, Harry 19
human, combustion, spontaneous 26

I
Indian, rope trick 20

J
Javor, Lazzlo 31
Johnson, Lady Bird 21
Jourdain, Eleanor 16
Jupiter, gravity on 9

K
Kamensky, Yuri 25
Karachi and Khydar 20
Katie the psychic 24
Kelly, Noah 19
kitten, winged 31

L
lake, monsters 30
Langton, Ron 28
largest known meteorite crater 8
Lee, John 33
lemons, deadly 16
Leonov, Alexei 10
letter B on Mars 12
Lincoln, Abraham 21
Loch Ness monster 31
Loft, Bob 16
Lost Dutchman Mine, Superstition Mountain, Arizona 30
Lucian of Samasota, Syria 7

M
magic and occult 15–21
   "abracadabra" 16
   American Spiritualist movement, origin of 16

Index

fortune telling 17
head, severed 20
Indian rope trick 20
lemons, deadly 16
photographs, ghostly 16, 21
poltergeist activity 15
testing for witches 16, 17
village, most haunted 21
Mandell, David 23
Mantell, Thomas 12
Mars, letter B on 12
Martian language 11
Maxwell, Greg Sheldon 16
Mercury's fast-moving year 9
meteorite 8
  crater, largest known 8
Michalak, Stephen 13
Miethe 13
Mikhaileva, Nelya 25
Miles, Sarah 29
Moberley, Charlotte Anne 16
Monroe, Mrs. Dora 21
monsters, lake 30
Moody, Rowland 28
moon 6–7, 10
  birth of the 6
  footprints on the 7
  gravity on the 6
  landing, early Chinese 7
Muller, Catherine 11
Mysterious Stranger 19
mystery creatures 29
myths and legends 28–31
  chupacabra footprint 31
  creatures, mystery 29
  kitten, winged 31
  lake monsters 30

N

Napoleon 22
Naumov, Edward 25
Nazca, Peru 33
Nazi flying discs 13
neutron stars 9, 10
Nikolatev, Karl 25
Nostradamus 22

O

occult see magic and occult
Operation Overlord 23
Orczy, Baroness 17
Ostmann, Albert 30

P

Palace of Versailles, France 16
Paul, Reverend Father of Moll 33
Peterson, Billy 26
Petta, Julia Buccola 33
Philolaus of Tarentum 8
photographs, ghostly 16, 21
Piddington, Sydney and Lesley 25
Pitchford, Richard Valentine 20
Plato 30
Pluckley, Britain 21
Pluto, gravity on 9
poltergeist activity 15
prophecies and coincidences 22–23
psychic, Katie the 24
Pullavar, Subbayah 20
puzzles and riddles 32–33
  trick of the eye 33

R

Reezer, Mrs. Mary 26
Rennie, James Alan 27
Repo, Don 16
Rhine, Professor 24
Rhodes, Rosie 29
riddles see puzzles and riddles
Roosevelt, Franklin D. 21
Roosevelt, Theodore 21
rope trick, Indian 20
Roswell, New Mexico 12
Russia, sighting of UFOs 14

S

Sack, Arthur 13
Salem witchcraft trial, Massachusetts 17
Saturn 10
Scheiner, Father 8
Schreiver 13
Schwarz, Dr. Berthold E. 24
Selbit, P.T. 20
Shepherd, Alan B. 10
Shipton, Eric 31
sighting of aliens 12
sighting of UFOs over Russia 14
Simon, Dr Benjamin 11
Simonton, Joe 11
Simpson, Mrs. 22
Skylab space station 10
Soyuz spaceship 10
space flight, first manned 9
spontaneous human combustion 26
Spring-Heeled Jack 31
Sputnik 1 7
St. Kevin 21
Stafford, Tom 10
stigmata 27
stone, cursed 30
stones, moving 28
Street of the Seven Devils, Jever, Germany 20
Sun 6, 8
  burning power of the 8
  statistics 6

T

Takhtarova, Anna and Rita 7
Taylor, Grant 24
Tereshkova, Valentina 10
testing for witches 16, 17
Towns, Captain 17
Trelfall, David 7
trick of the eye 33
trick, Indian rope 20
Trindade Island, South Atlantic 12
Triumph® International Japan 19
Truman, Harry S 21
Turin Shroud 33
Tutankhamun's tomb 22

U

UFOs 11–14
  "flying saucer," origin of 13
  flying saucer experiment 12
  Nazi flying discs 13
  photographic evidence 13
  sighting over Russia 14
  UFO, burns from 13
  see also aliens
unexplained phenomena 26–28
  age of the universe 8
  America's first manned space flight 10
  American/Russian meeting in space 10
  Barringer crater, Arizona 8
  black hole formation 8
  comets 9
  craft, missing 27
  crop circles 28
  earth measurements 9
  eclipse and the discovery of America 10
  fish in space, first 9
  Jupiter, gravity on 9
  manned space flight, first 9
  Mercury's year 9
  meteorite crater, largest known 8
  Moon landing, early Chinese 7
  Moon
    birth of the 6
    footprints on the 7
    gravity on the 6
    statistics 6
  neutron stars 9, 10
  Pluto, gravity on 9
  showers, unusual 28
  singing "Happy Birthday" in space 10
  spontaneous human combustion 26
  stigmata 27
  stones, moving 28

Index

Sun statistics 6
Sun, burning power of the 6
universe 6–10

V
Valentino, Rudolph 28
Villa, Paul 13
village, most haunted 21
Vostok 1 10

W
War of the Worlds 11
Washington Cathedral 7
Webster, Ken 15
Welles, Orson 11
Wells, H.G. 11
White, John 31
Wilhelmina, Queen of the Netherlands 21
William the Conqueror 23
Winchester Mystery House 32
Winchester, Sarah 32
witches, testing for 16, 17
World War I 22, 31
World War II 23
Worth, Patience 16

Y
Yeti footprint 30
Yeti hand 31
Yorke, Carson 14
Yowie, sketch of the 30

ACKNOWLEDGMENTS

Jacket (b/l) Ken McKay/Rex Features; (t/r) Rex Features

9 (b) ITD/REX; 10 (t) AFP/GETTYIMAGE; 11 (l) FPL; 12 (t) Emanuel Ilan/AFP/GETTYIMAGE, (b) FPL; 13 (t) Paul Villa/FPL, (b) Mary Evans Picture Library; 14 (t) FPL, (b) Sipa Press/REX; 15 (t) Ken Webster/FPL, (b) Ken Webster/FPL; 16 (t) FPL, (b) Marina Jackson/FPL; 17 (b) FPL; 18 (t) Doug Kanter/AFP/GETTYIMAGE, (b) Matt Cambell/AFP/GETTYIMAGE; 19 (c/l) Carl de Souza/AFP/GETTYIMAGE, (t) Rus/Rex, (b) Nicolas Asfouri/AFP/GETTYIMAGE; 20 (t/r) FPL, (b) FPL; 21 (t) E. Coxon/FPL; 22 (r) Hulton-Deutsch Collection/CORBIS; 23 (b) ZZ/XXH/SPL/REX; 24 (c) Dr. B. E. Schwarz/FPL; 25 (t/l) Kevin Braithwaite/FPL, (r) Ken McKay/REX, (b) Saeed Khan/APF/GETTYIMAGE; 26 (r) Larry E. Arnold/FPL; 27 (b/r) Dr. Elmar R. Gruber/FPL, (b/l) Dr. Elmar R. Gruber/FPL; 28 (t) FPL, (b) FPL; 29 (t) SWS/REX, (b) SWS/REX; 30 (t) Cliff Crook/FPL, (b) Tony Healy/FPL; 31 (c) FPL, (b) Tony Healy/FPL; 32 (c/l) Charles Sykes/REX, (b) Charles Sykes/REX; 33 (t/l) FPL

FPL – Fortean Picture Library

All other photos are from Corel, PhotoDisc, Digital Vision and Ripley's Entertainment Inc.

Anderson Public Library
Lawrenceburg, KY 40342